Successful Fundraising and Sponsorship
in a week

Sue McKoen

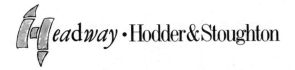

Headway · Hodder & Stoughton

Acknowledgement

Thank you to Steve Morris for his inspiration and encouragement.

Cataloguing in Publication Data is available from the British Library.

ISBN 0 340 67925 5

First published 1997
Impression number   10   9   8   7   6   5   4   3   2   1
Year   1999   1998   1997

Copyright © 1997 Sue McKoen

All rights reserved. No part of this publication may be
reproduced or transmitted in any form or by any means,
electronic or mechanical, including photocopy, recording, or
any information storage and retrieval system, without
permission in writing from the publisher or under licence
from the Copyright Licensing Agency Limited. Further
details of such licences (for reprographic reproduction) may
be obtained from the Copyright Licensing Agency Limited, of
90 Tottenham Court Road, London W1P 9HE.

Typeset by Multiplex Techniques Ltd, St Mary Cray, Kent.
Printed in Great Britain for Hodder & Stoughton Educational,
a division of Hodder Headline Plc, 338 Euston Road,
London NW1 3BH by Cox & Wyman Ltd, Reading.

the Institute of Management

FOUNDATION

The Institute of Management (IM) is at the forefront of management development and best management practice. The Institute embraces all levels of management from students to chief executives. It provides a unique portfolio of services for all managers, enabling them to develop skills and achieve management excellence.

For information on the benefits of membership, please contact:

Department HS
Institute of Management
Cottingham Road
Corby
Northants NN17 1TT
Tel: 01536 204222
Fax: 01536 201651

This series is commissioned by the Institute of Management Foundation.

C O N T E N T S

Fundraising gets emotional – for charities and donors alike. Charities depend on funding to carry on their work, but raising money can be an uphill struggle. The recession, cuts in government funding and the sheer number of new charities starting up each year, are making it harder and harder for good causes to raise the money they need.

It's tough for donors too. Their letter boxes are overflowing with deserving appeals, all tugging at the heart strings (not to mention the purse strings). It's impossible to give to them all – even if you're a millionaire!

Fundraising (by charities or groups running special projects) has come a long way since the heady days of the 1980s. Then, all most charities had to do was ask and a cheque dropped magically into their laps. Today, appeals for funds must do more than tug at the heart strings – they must stand out from the crowd and make sound business sense. Especially appeals to the corporate sector, which gives billions of pounds worth of support worldwide every year.

So how can you get a head start in the great fundraising race? This book gives fundraisers a practical, step by step guide to asking companies for that all important funding. It's written from the fundraiser's viewpoint – but remember that most successful fundraising and sponsorship deals are partnerships between the donor and receiver. So managers giving out company funds can also use this book, as a guide to what to expect from the organisation appealing to them.

The steps you will work through are:

- deciding whether or not to raise funds – is it the right approach/solution?
- prioritising your needs
- proving the unique appeal of your cause
- looking at the funding options – from donations to sponsorships
- how to spot a potential funder
- what to find out before asking for money
- putting together a convincing proposal – one that will grab the donor's attention and not just get filed in the bin!
- waiting for the answer
- making the most of your efforts (whether or not you get funding)

Your week looks like this.

Sunday	I need money!
Monday	The proof, Mr Watson
Tuesday	How can I raise funds?
Wednesday	Spotting a donor
Thursday	Putting together your appeal
Friday	Decisions, decisions
Saturday	Making the most of your week

I need money!

Today you have a brain wave – how to fund that pipe-dream project.

> *I'll just ask Bloggs & Co down the road – it's a big company, they're bound to have a few thousand pounds to donate. After all, it's a really important project.*

Stop right there! Once in a while, fundraisers get lucky and raise the money they need simply by asking. Sadly, as a general rule, raising funds takes a great deal more time and effort than pulling a rabbit clutching a corporate cheque out of a hat!

No matter who you are raising funds for – a charity, education, health or arts organisation, welfare or other special interests group, large or small (the list is endless) – you need to think carefully before picking up the phone or writing an appeal letter. It's not the actual asking that takes time, it's being sure what you should ask for.

Some crucial questions

Ask yourself the following questions – and be really honest about the answers :

- What do you want to ask for?
- Why do you need it?
- Why should a donor give it to you?

Doubtless you are convinced by your answers. But would you convince your bank manager?

Today we'll examine the general issues you should consider before setting off down the fundraising road. On Monday we'll discover what is (or maybe isn't) appealing about your project. Then we'll re-visit these questions. You may find your answers change – but by Tuesday you should be confident enough to confront the Chief Executive of Bloggs & Co, and your bank manager there and then!

A few definitions

Just to avoid confusion, we're going to stick to certain names for the people and processes involved in fundraising.

- **The fundraiser** – you, the person seeking a donation, sponsorship or any other sort of funding
- **The project** – the specific thing you need to fund – a building, salary, event, publication, even on-going work
- **The cause** – the general issue your charity or group works to support or solve

- **The donor** – the person you hope will sponsor or fund your project. We'll look at this who's who of givers on Wednesday

A few home truths

Fundraisers need to be convincing – if you don't sound totally convinced by your cause, nobody else will be. Anyone who has rattled a donations can on a street corner, or negotiated a high level corporate sponsorship, knows the prospect donor will only sign that cheque if they are utterly confident that your cause is worthwhile. Just because you're committed to the cause, doesn't mean that they will share your passion.

Step back from your project and put yourself firmly in the donor's shoes. Think of fundraising like buying a treat at a market stall – you don't really need it, but the stall holder is so convincing that you just can't resist. As you work through this book, deciding how to make your appeal, keep asking yourself:

* What am I selling the donor?
* Why should they want to buy it?

There are lots of different answers to these questions, often not the obvious ones that immediately strike you. Contrary to vicious rumour, philanthropy isn't entirely dead! Numerous companies still support good causes because they feel they should. Others support charity because it makes good business sense – a way to get closer to the charity's supporters who may be prospective customers, or a means of adding perceived value to a product. Today, corporate giving is often a combination of philanthropy and business acumen.

Either way, most companies will expect the fundraiser to convince them that giving support is a good commercial decision. This is not simply because that is the way good business deals are created. Any director who agrees to fund a project is likely to have to prove to senior colleagues or Board members why support for that cause was a good idea. After all, no business wants to pour money into a black hole never to see it do any good. Take two examples:

The corporate philanthropist
The Co-operative Bank's Managing Director Terry Thomas knows exactly why the bank supports charity.

> *We genuinely believe that profitability and principles go hand in hand. And it is something our customers expect us to do.*

Corporate philanthropy was a guiding principle for the Co-op Bank when it was founded in the 1890s, and it still holds true today. The bank's advertising campaigns highlight their ethical concerns. As a recent Co-op advert states:

> *We absolutely refuse to invest our customers' money in companies that needlessly damage the environment or exploit animals. Nor will we do business with countries that deny people basic human rights.*

This is now something of a unique selling feature for the Co-op which their customers value greatly.

The promotional donor
Rank Hovis McDougall Foods also believes supporting charity is a good thing. According to RHM's marketing controller Susan Millington

> *A charity link is no longer just a gesture of goodwill – it also makes good business sense.*

In one promotional deal, RHM linked their Bisto gravy brand with the National Society for the Prevention of Cruelty to Children (NSPCC), producing a charity cookbook. RHM felt the NSPCC complemented the image of Bisto – with its smiling children logo. The promotion raised well over £150,000 for the NSPCC. RHM also experienced a major effect on Bisto sales at a peak trading time, which they happily attributed to the promotion.

What can fundraising really do for you?

All those who answered 'Give me stacks of cash to run my pet project' please go to the bottom of the class immediately!

Deciding to raise funds can do lots of things for you and your cause ... some surprisingly pleasant, not all of them entirely enjoyable!

So what are the good bits? Fundraising can

- raise the vital cash you need and so
- ensure your project goes ahead or continues
- help to get lots more people involved in your cause. People who might not wish to commit themselves exclusively to your cause as full time volunteers may support fundraising efforts for a fixed period of time – a year or 18 months perhaps
- widen your appeal – every new person who becomes involved has a network of friends and colleagues who they may be able to interest in your cause too. That can lead you to unexpected heights – as the saying goes, there are only ever seven people between you and the President of the United States

- raise the profile of your cause – fundraising and events can make appealing press stories. We'll look at making the most of the media on Saturday
- help you nurture donors for the future. Once on board, you can work to build a positive relationship with the donor, reporting on what their money is helping to achieve throughout the project. They'll only continue to give if they want to, but this nurturing period provides an invaluable opportunity

And the bad bits? Fundraising

- creates a great deal of extra work – planning, courting donors, managing volunteers, arranging events or sponsorship benefits – the list is endless
- costs money – most fundraisers reckon a fundraising drive will cost anywhere between 2-5% of the money raised, depending on the size of the appeal. Some large appeals for millions cost even

more – the London School of Economics estimated their Second Century Campaign to raise £40 million would cost around 10% of the money they raised

- loses you sleep – a fundraising campaign is a full time job. Some donors pursue a hands off approach – others call with incessant queries at all times of the day and night! Fundraisers must respond with charm and speed, even if it means working through the night. However, don't become a slave! Even in fundraising, you'll meet the odd time waster who will never end up supporting your cause, no matter how keen they seem (more on this on Friday)

- means planning for the future – if a donor gives now, they may feel they've done their bit when your next fundraising appeal comes around in 12 months' time. So plan ahead – do you want the donor to give now or later?

- means lots of thank you letters – it's crucial to say thank you if you want to keep donors friendly, no matter how large or small their support. If you hate writing thank you letters for your Christmas presents, beware!

- takes time – planning, contacting potential donors, waiting for company charity boards to meet all takes time. Rushing things can often be fatal, so be prepared to wait

Don't be put off. Good planning at this stage will save a lot of headaches later. It's also amazing the energy and adrenaline rush you get from believing you're close to raising the money you need.

The corporate view

There are pros and cons for corporate donors too. On the positive side, supporting charity means enabling them to do something they otherwise couldn't. It can be a tax efficient way of handling company profits. There are potential PR and marketing benefits from association with a good cause, creating a positive public image. This is not only good in terms of media coverage, but can also help win the hearts of new customer segments.

Corporate support for charity is a good way of boosting staff morale, through incentive schemes or team fundraising events. Just look at how many companies have thrown themselves into the Comic Relief Red Nose Days. Allied Dunbar are one of the many companies who have used charitable support as a management training scheme. They sent teams of managers to help the National Trust with land management on their properties, from maintaining woodlands to dry stone wall building.

Sadly, there can be a down side too. Both funder and cause need to take care when choosing to form a funding partnership. If they are ill matched it can lead to adverse PR, and problems for all concerned. The National Trust accepted a donation from British Coal when controversy over the company's land fill sites was rife. The media reaction to the donation was caustic to say the least!

A little self analysis

Now that you have thought about the sort of donor you have to convince, and some of the bonuses and pitfalls of fundraising, it's time to put your cause and project under the microscope.

Your current situation will have a strong impact on what you can realistically achieve. Putting together a multi-million pound sponsorship package as an unknown one-man-band charity is probably a tad ambitious! On the other hand, fundraising is all about determination and not always accepting no for an answer: finding the right project to interest the right prospective funders and getting the result you need. So think positive and don't give up!

Where am I now? – Resources

Look at the following list of resources and jot down your own answers on a piece of paper:

People
How many people work for your cause? How much time could they dedicate to your fundraising drive? Are there any volunteers you could get involved?

The scale of fundraising you decide to take on, will depend upon the resources you have at your disposal.

Space
How much space will you need? What type of space – an office; storage; venue, indoors or out? Raising a donation for on-going work may just require a telephone, a word processor and a desk. Whereas an event probably needs a venue, co-ordination centre, working space for volunteers and storage.

Look at what's available. Decide if you can adapt it. If not, can you borrow a spare room in a local office or volunteer's house? Or maybe ask the prospect donor for help?

Support

Like any other job, fundraising means using and paying for administration and the materials to do the job: photocopying, phones and post, even the coffee supply to keep you bright-eyed through the wee small hours. Such added extras are all too easy to ignore, but if you plan to use existing office facilities, you're costing your office money. In fact, it's terrifying how the overheads can mount up if you don't plan ahead for them.

It's sensible to raise money to cover these overheads, so project roughly what they will cost over the fundraising period. But beware – some companies and trusts won't fund administration costs.

Where am I now? – Funding

Now do the same for funding.

How are you funded now?
If you've already done some fundraising, think about what worked out and what didn't. Could it be time to try a new approach?

Fundraising is surprisingly susceptible to fashionable trends. Glitzy events were all the rage in the booming 80s; the recession hit and events lost their appeal. Now more and more charities raise funds through employee schemes, endorsement deals or on-pack promotions – we'll look at these on Tuesday.

It's never too late to try something new – The Chicken Shed Theatre is one of London's most successful fringe theatre groups, a regular award winner for their innovative fundraising efforts. They started seeking corporate sponsorship in 1995 after 20 years of fundraising from trusts and donations.

What happened with past fundraising efforts?
Learn from your history and check there aren't any fundraising skeletons in the cupboard. Discover what your predecessors have tried, what worked and what didn't. It's worth doing this research carefully, both to save yourself re-inventing the wheel, and to pick up any handy contacts and hints you may be able to use again.

If you're new to fundraising
Think now about just how much time and effort you are willing to commit to raising money.

You can do it yourself, but consider whether it's time to call in the professionals. Someone with a track record as a professional fundraiser, or a volunteer who knows the fundraising ropes, could save you a lot of time and effort searching for the right approach and contacts. Get in touch with the professional body representing fundraisers or voluntary organisations, and ask if they have a list of reputable freelance fundraisers or consultants.

Alternatively, do you know of any volunteers who have successfully raised money for good causes who might help you out? Check them out first before asking for help. You'll still need to support and co-ordinate all their fundraising efforts, but at least you can delegate some of the hard work.

Where am I now? – causes and pipe-dreams

Finally, think about what your cause stands for and your plans for the future.

Sex appeal

Strange though it may sound, sex appeal is crucial! Some causes just don't have any sex appeal. Maybe it's a subject people don't like to talk about, it turns their stomach, or is just a little too close to home.

Subjects like drug abuse or homelessness can be depressing, and not something with which a sponsor will comfortably associate publicly. Others are just dead boring – a seaweed survey is unlikely to attract hoards of day trippers or the press! Think of it another way – unhealthy seaweed can reveal problems which have a huge impact on preserving marine life, including cute and cuddly seals.

It's all in the packaging – serious and unpalatable facts can still be driven home by telling them in a different way. So think about how to sell your cause positively. Focus on solutions, highlight past successes (something you can repeat if you get the funding). Think laterally!

Moral issues

What type of corporate donor and fundraising are you willing to be associated with? Some may make very unsuitable bedfellows – would you expect a human rights campaign to be sponsored by a major trader with an oppressive regime?

Think about the blood money factor too, as Trevor Griffiths of the RNIB explains

> *We're not going to deal with a company that contradicts the aims of the charity – that would be pretty short sighted. Even if you receive a substantial sum of money, you also confuse the public, upset clients and could well lose far more in the long run.*

Some companies aim to redress the negative impact of their commercial activity by supporting charities solving these problems. Things are rarely black and white though. National Children's Homes linking up with a solvent manufacturer might seem inappropriate – but what if the aim is to work together to help prevent solvent abuse?

Make sure you choose a donor and a method which fits your style of cause.

Plans

What plans does your charity have? One of the things you may have to produce to persuade companies to fund you, is a business plan. It doesn't have to be a glossy tome, simply something that shows clearly that you've thought about what you need to do, long and short term, know how to go about achieving it and how much it will cost you.

What does your cause want to do, now and in five years time? Is the project you want to fund a key part of these plans? What other projects do you need to undertake? Be really honest about this and remember, just because it's a good idea doesn't necessarily mean you need to do it.

Emerging from the analyst's couch

By now you should have a pretty good idea as to whether or not this morning's brain wave of raising funds for your pet project is a good idea.

Maybe you now think fundraising isn't right! Maybe you've found you don't really need to raise money or that the project doesn't really need to go ahead?

If you still think your project is crucial, write down three good reasons why it needs to happen.

Summary

Today you have looked at:

- the pros and cons of fundraising
- why companies support good causes

and identified

- where you are now
- what you want to do
- all the issues you'll need to deal with to have the best chance of raising funds successfully

So finally, here's a checklist to take you onto tomorrow.

Checklist

- What do you want to do and why?
- Check what resources you can use to help you raise funds
- Think about administration costs
- Check who funds you now
- Check what fundraising has been done in the past
- Consider if help from an experienced fundraiser would be useful
- Know your moral limits!

And throughout it all keep asking yourself:

- What am I selling?
- Why might a donor be interested?

The proof, Mr Watson!

Now that you've decided fundraising is the right course of action, it's time to get down to some detailed planning.

Today we look at your cause and chosen project in more detail, and start pulling together the arguments you'll use to convince prospective donors that yours is the cause for them. By tomorrow you'll have the basic facts and figures that prove why your project is important and needs support. You'll also identify the generic Unique Selling Point (USP) – the factor that makes your project special to everyone affected by it, including the funder.

Do I have the project for you!

Time for a little market research. It may seem obvious to you that your project needs funding, but do you really know why? Ask yourself the following fundamental questions. You'll need to do this even if you're trying to fund the on-going work of your cause. Try to give short answers – a few lines each.

- What is your cause?
- Why is it important?
- What project do you want to fund?
- Why is the project needed?
- Why do you need funding to support it?
- What would happen if you got no funding?
- What happens when you've spent the money you've raised?

Just to put things into perspective, let's look at a couple of examples.

Imagine the Queen the day after Windsor Castle burnt down. Her Majesty's answers could be as simple as this:

- My Castle and I
- One does need somewhere to live
- Rebuilding one's castle
- Well, there was this conservator, a bottle of terps and .... boom!
- The Royal purse is a little bare this year – £8 million in loose change is beyond even our means
- One's American subjects would be so disappointed
- The tourists will return. Then one can start earning the money to pay one's tax bill

Alternatively, try a less extreme example.

An environmental campaign
A fundraiser working for an environmental group needs to raise money. It's to support a campaign to ban the trade in endangered species. Every year millions of rare animals and birds are taken from the wild to supply pet shops. Some countries have banned this trade, but others haven't. It's a highly profitable business, so millions of endangered creatures are still trapped and smuggled abroad each year. Transported in appalling conditions, many die of starvation, disease, overcrowding or exhaustion. The facts are pretty gruesome.

- What is your cause?
  - To protect the environment and its wildlife
- Why is it important?
  - We're destroying the environment alarmingly fast – if we fail to protect it now, we'll lose it forever
- What project do you want to fund?
  - A campaign to ban the international trade in wild animals and birds
- Why is it needed?
  - To persuade governments to pass laws stopping the import, suffering and death of millions of rare wild animals and birds every year
- Why do you need funding to support it?
  - To lobby governments in the UK and overseas; raise awareness in the media; and fund undercover operations to catch poachers
- What would happen if you got no funding?
  - We'd carry on campaigning – but it would take years to do what needs to be done now!
- What happens when you've spent the money you've raised?
  - We've budgeted for a year's work – it should take 6-12 months to do everything planned. We'll review things in 6 months and, presuming we've reached the goals we should have by then, raise more money if needed

Over to you

If you're concerned about the environment you'll probably be swayed by these answers. The same applies if you're trying to rebuild the church roof, pay for an extra staff member, fund research into splitting the atom or sponsor a glamorous fundraising ball for orphaned children. Oh, and on-going work too – your answers may be a little more general, but they still need to convince people.

It's not a matter of trying to catch you out, just that any company will want to know that their investment will achieve something. That you, the charity, have thought through all aspects of the project in a business-like fashion. Otherwise they may as well build a bonfire of £50 notes in the company car park!

Preparing for action

What plans do you make to go on holiday? Look at the brochure; choose an African safari; book the ticket. What about a tent? Will there be enough mosquito repellent? And don't forget to take lots of film … there isn't a Boots in the African bush! Cancel the papers, get someone to feed the cat. Oh, and Aunty Enid is coming to tea next Thursday? Better cancel her too. Forget these details and you'll come home bitten to death, with no photo of that charging rhino, to find a very grumpy cat, and Aunty Enid sitting on your doorstep ready to disinherit you.

Planning to raise funds is the same. Fail to work through all the details now, you'll get caught unawares later. It could mean the difference between securing a sponsorship deal and your project becoming a distant dream.

Planning your project

One of the best ways to think through your plans is to have a brainstorming session. Call together everyone involved in the project – planning it now and running it afterwards. If you're trying to fund an on-going work programme you may already have a five year business plan. If not, use this process to help you start producing one – you will need it!

At this stage just concentrate on the project – the fundraising plan comes next. These steps may help you plan the meeting.

Step 1 List the project's objectives
Step 2 Make a timetable – are there any deadline dates?
Step 3 What are the milestones – things that need to happen in a certain order before moving onto the next stage?
Step 4 What about external factors – are there other projects, plans or people, in-house or outside that need considering?
Step 5 List the resources that are in place already – including funds if any

Work through every step of the project logically drawing up a basic guide as to what needs doing. Nothing is too silly to think about at this stage, but try to keep the final plan to a basic skeleton of the main facts and milestones. Fundraising will be one of these milestones.

Bomb detection

Every project plan will throw up more problems to think about and plan. Look for the hidden bombs now. Tasks you haven't anticipated, lack of staff time, conflicting pressures from other projects, work other good causes are doing which may conflict with or negate what you are planning. Look back at the resources list you made on Sunday to prompt your thoughts.

Hunting for the USP

Whatever you are fundraising for, you need to identify the Unique Selling Point. What is it about your cause and project that will be uniquely appealing to a donor? It's especially crucial if your cause is not that well known – if companies have to ask 'who are you?' or 'what do you do?'

Start with your cause. Most good causes will already have a mission statement or rally call defining what they are about. Take the following care charities' explanatory strap lines – explanatory slogans that always accompany the charity's title or logo:

- British Red Cross – Caring for people in crisis
- RNIB – Challenging blindness
- MENCAP – Making the most of life

It could just be as simple as Save our Church Hall/Village Pond.

Now look at your project. What makes it special? No matter what you are dealing with, there will be some reason that makes your project unique to the companies to which you are appealing. Approach this exercise thinking that your project is not that special and you'll fall at the first fundraising fence.

Stuck for ideas? Look at what other good causes are saying – especially those similar to your own – then adapt these ideas ... but be original! Run a competition asking staff, or supporters familiar with your project, for ideas. Ask everyone in your brainstorming session to come up with five words or a short phrase to sum up the importance of your project. These thought starters may get your imagination churning!

USP thought starters

The church roof – the last remaining Saxon church tower in Hertfordshire

St Bartholemew's Hospital – the oldest teaching hospital in London

An AIDS advice centre – the busiest AIDS advice centre in Glasgow servicing thousands of people

Blindness – in 1995 the RNIB challenged Anneka Rice of the TV programme *Challenge Anneka* to help them build the world's first sensory maze at their residential college in Worcester

Checking your argument

Double check if your argument is water tight with some market research. Ask a friend or colleague who is not involved in your cause to be your guinea-pig and test your answers out, especially your USP. If you can, ask someone who is a company director, or better still, who handles company donations. You'll know who you can trust and talk to openly.

Listen to their advice and review all your answers. You'll need to review them again once you've pinpointed who to ask for support – we'll look at this on Thursday.

Budgets

Proving the need is one thing – costing it is quite another. The budget is the bottom line for any fundraising approach: the facts that lay out clearly how you will spend the donor's money. Real budgets need thought – so avoid the back of a napkin in the restaurant approach. Claret may have helped Chancellor Norman Lamont tot up the figures, but your hangover will be far worse when you discover you've forgotten hundreds of pounds of costs!

Your project plan should make it fairly straightforward to attribute costs. Split the budget up into manageable chunks such as salaries, materials, equipment, administration and so on, according to what you're going to spend most money on. There are no hard and fast rules, but the following hints may help.

Do

- **keep it simple** – a donor will want to see an outline budget, not all the costings down to the last paper clip. Of course, you'll need to track your costs very thoroughly, but at this stage go for sensible ball park figures
- **get quotes** – if you're buying or hiring equipment, contracting services, even getting other internal departments to do work for you, ask them to quote for their work so the bills don't come as a shock

- **check past projects** – if you've done anything similar before, check how accurate these past budgets were. If not, try getting advice from another party who has already done what you are planning
- **add a contingency figure** – there are always hidden extras on any project, things you can't predict, especially if you're tackling a new type of project. Building contractors commonly budget for a 25% increase in costs; 5-10% is probably more reasonable, depending on how accurately points 1-3 have enabled you to cost things
- **show potential savings** – indicate where savings on one part of the budget will reduce costs elsewhere, to show you've really thought through the options. For example getting a DTP package now might mean you could do all your publicity far cheaper in-house

Don't

- **get by on a shoestring** – tying things together with string when you really need rope is a lost cause! Getting by on the bare minimum, when asking for a little bit more would make all the difference, isn't a virtue
- **forget the hidden costs** – everything from paper clips and coffee to postage, telephone calls and internal staff time
- **bump up the costs** – companies know very well how much things cost, so don't be tempted to create fantastical budgets. Many companies will pay donations against receipts, so the accountant will catch up with you!

- **economise** – don't quote bargain basement prices either. Quote the real price. If you manage to get a great deal later, that's an added bonus. Then ask if you can use the money you've saved to purchase something else
- **forget what's been funded already** – indicating the money you've raised already on the budget demonstrates success. Donors are often coy about being the first person to support a cause – joining the party is easier

Summary

Today, you put your cause and project under the microscope. You should now have some very good reasons why your project needs to happen and deserves to get corporate support. Looking back at the answer you gave on Sunday morning may tell you a few things about the way you perceived your cause/project before you started to look at it objectively.

You are now well on the way to developing your appeal. Tomorrow is a new day.

How can I raise funds?

The fundamental rule when choosing a fundraising approach is to stick with methods you can deliver. Stay realistic at all times and avoid promising yourself, and the prospect donor, the earth.

Today you'll think through various fundraising approaches and decide on your next step. This is not navel contemplation – it's crucial to think things through now before rushing off to organise something… otherwise it can all go horribly wrong.

Different types of fundraising will mean watching out for different pitfalls. You also need to get to grips with various tax and VAT rules which can work for or very much against you.

Here we'll just consider the mainstream techniques. There are lots of specialist techniques – such as direct mail, catalogue sales, lotteries and telephone fundraising – requiring specialist knowledge, which fall outside the realms of this book. If you get to Saturday and want to investigate some of these, there's a short book list to help you find out more.

Rattling cans

Collecting donations on street corners or door to door is undoubtedly a very effective way to raise funds – but not something we're going to cover here.

However, a swift word of caution. If you want to don a silly costume, stick a charity logo on a bucket and chase shoppers down the high street, you (and your charity) need a licence and permission to do it on a certain day or time. Regulations vary from place to place, so check with the charity you're raising for or your local authority first before putting on that panda suit.

By the way, don't even think of collecting money in public if you are not a registered charity – it's straightforward begging and your local policeman won't take too kindly to it.

A guided tour

Here is a guide to some of the ways you can raise money from companies.

Sponsorship

The company supports your project in return for promotional recognition to benefit the company's trade: a business expense.

Example

The Cadburys Save the Children Strollerthon.

Pros

- **High profile** – all about getting the corporate logo seen – on products, in the media, in front of an audience, anywhere you can imagine it! The cause and the sponsor get exposure in front of the audience they want to reach
- **More money** – you can charge more for sponsorship than just cost because of the added benefits the company gets. The most important benefit is association with your cause – through your logo and the associated feel good factor
- **Corporation tax relief** (company Income Tax) – presuming the company gets reasonable benefits for the amount of sponsorship paid (if not, the tax man can disallow it)

The Panda Picnic

Imagine Fiat pay WWF £20,000 to sponsor a fundraising Panda Picnic in the Park. When they come to pay Corporation tax on £2 million profits at the end of the year Fiat could deduct the £20,000 sponsorship from their recorded profits and only pay tax on £1,980,000. Great value!

Cons

- **VAT** – your charity provides a business service, promoting the sponsoring company, so payments are VATable

- not a problem if both your cause and the sponsoring company are VAT registered. Simply invoice the company for sponsorship + VAT; the company then offsets the sponsorship VAT against its own VAT bill from sales
- a potential problem if the sponsor isn't VAT registered. They may object to paying the extra

- **Providing sponsor benefits** – unlike a donation the sponsor receives benefits in return for funding your project. These need to be reasonable in relation to the sponsorship price, so don't go offering free trips to your project in the Bahamas if the sponsorship is only small change

Exclusions

Sponsorship stops being an allowable business expense if the money is used for capital expenditure e.g. for the construction of a building. You can name the building after the sponsor, but the payment must be a <u>donation</u> (see below) and can't be set against Corporation Tax.

Is it for you?

Why not? If you have the resources to manage it and your project can attract the audience and public attention the company wants. Generally better suited to events or objects such as publications.

Sponsorship is increasingly popular but decide what you can deliver – without tearing your hair out. Would a donation be simpler and more cost effective?

Endorsements and promotions

Commercial partnership where the company promotes goods or services alongside the charity name.

Endorsement
Your cause's logo or name is used to show approval for a product, perhaps in exchange for an annual fee or a percentage of the sale price. So the RSPCA might endorse certain pet foods; an AIDS charity, a brand of condom.

Promotion
A bit more up front, mostly involving larger sums of money. Promotions build stronger links between the charity, product and consumer, via competitions or special product offers (collect 20 tokens and get a cuddly toy/ reduced rate membership). Some promotions also raise xp for every product or service bought, usually towards a minimum guaranteed donation.

Examples
Browse along the shelves of your local supermarket – especially the cereals, biscuits, drinks and pet food.

Pros
- **Profile** – hit upon the right commercial partnership, everyone wins. The charity gets added exposure via advertising, on-pack information and being seen wherever the product is sold. The company gains added value from being seen to support the charity, a good additional PR slant

- **The right audience** – with the right partnership supporters and the product's consumers should be a good match, interested in both the product and the cause. Promotions/endorsements help companies boost existing customer loyalty and find new customers. Charity supporters are more likely to buy products favoured by their pet cause, and new supporters become aware of the charity via the product, all helping to raise funds. A good symbiotic relationship

Cons
- **Usually taxable** – but not always with endorsements, where the charity provides nothing material in return for the donations. Check the latest regulations with the Inland Revenue
- **The wrong audience** – get your market research wrong, nobody likes the product or link-up, everyone's unhappy and you're left with hundreds of mouldering cereal packets on the shelves!

A reminder
By law you must ensure any endorsed or promotional product (and the material supporting it – leaflets, ads etc.) states clearly that your cause is a charity and how it will benefit. A recent cereal promotion between supermarket chain Tesco and WWF stated this information like this: *For every pack sold, Tesco will donate 5p with a minimum guaranteed donation of £100,000 to WWF-UK a registered charity Number 201707.*

You'll see this standard wording on lots of promotions – for the time being it should keep your promotion within the law!

Is it for you?

If your cause has sex appeal, yes. Promotions tend to perform less well in times of recession when the consumer's prime concern is value for money, rather than fun widgets.

Formalise all the details as early as possible in a contract or business agreement letter (see Friday). It focuses the mind, and will help avoid costly and embarrassing attempts to extract yourself from a commercial partnership that doesn't look so beneficial in the light of day.

Donations

Exactly that, a gift freely given with no strings – well almost!

Many companies give donations via their **Charitable Trust Funds** – charities set up from company profits distributing annual interest earnings as charitable gifts. Others donate a proportion of the annual profits, match employees fundraising or give gifts in kind (see below).

Grants are donations or interest free loans, made by government departments or non-governmental agencies like the National Rivers Authority.

Example

The Co-operative Bank aim to give around 2% of their annual profits to charity – they even run a customer ballot for Gold credit card holders to nominate charities they want the bank to support.

Pros

- **Tax relief** – a company can get tax relief on gifts totalling up to 3% of the value of their ordinary share dividends each year. Charities can claim back basic rate tax on all donations – more if the gift is given tax effectively (see Gift Aid and Covenants)
- **Less hassle** – it still takes time to ask, but then all you need to do is say thank you and keep the donor informed of how their support is helping – a great way to build a long term relationship

Cons

- **No company promotion benefits** – advertising, promoting logos and products are not allowed (otherwise it becomes a taxable sponsorship) although you should say thank you whenever you reasonably can
- **Donations criteria** – a pro and a con. Donors know what they are willing to fund and most companies publish details of their giving criteria. However, not all companies are terribly clear about what they will and won't fund, so .... We'll look at this tomorrow

A reminder

Trust funds have strict pre-determined purposes which they can fund, which can't be changed other than by an act of Parliament. If a Trust says they only fund one-legged hermits in Tibet, they probably can't even fund two-legged Tibetan hermits. Call to ask, but in general don't waste their time applying.

Is it for you?

Perhaps the safest approach for new fundraisers – that doesn't mean the money will fall out of trees, but at least thorough research should point you in the right direction. But remember there's a lot of competition for donations.

Gift Aid and Covenants

Make the most of company donations by making them tax efficient* via:

Gift Aid – for donations over £250 net each.

It works like this – Bloggs & Co donate £1,000 gross to the local hospice, who suggest they sign a Gift Aid form (available from the tax man). That way Bloggs & Co deduct basic rate income tax (24%) from their donation and pay £760. The charity reclaims the remaining £240 from the tax man. If Bloggs & Co pay higher rate tax they also get tax relief on that higher amount (another £160 in this case). So Bloggs & Co would spend £600 to give the Hospice £1,000

or

Covenants

Where the company commits to a set annual donation over 4 years or more. Tax relief works the same way as Gift Aid but Bloggs & Co have to notify you if they want to stop giving.

* We've quoted the tax rates at the time of writing – check for any changes.

Gifts in kind

Some companies prefer to support charity by giving goods rather than money – many do both. It will cost a computer or a minibus manufacturer a good deal less to donate their product than it would for you to buy it.

Example
The Big Issue is a charity which helps the homeless through the sale (by homeless street vendors) of their eponymous magazine. It keeps running costs to a bare minimum with gifts in kind. Stationery, equipment, furniture and even the articles in their magazine are all donated, ensuring the maximum possible benefit for the homeless.

Pros

- **Tapping into stock** – it's not just production stock from manufacturers. Lots of companies dispose of unwanted office furniture and equipment which can really help charities. Ford UK give their old office furniture and storage units to schools, hospitals and charities local to their headquarters in Brentwood, Essex
- **Space** – borrowing an office or storage space can also be a gift in kind. The RSPB (based in Bedfordshire) ran a fundraising ballet gala at the Royal Opera House in London from an office in the basement of an estate agents in West London … rent free
- **Charity auctions** – sales of donated goods are not considered to be trading, so the profits aren't taxable. So gifts in kind can also be used as lots for charity auctions

Cons

- **What you see is what you get** – you can't afford to be picky. Gifts are unlikely to be state of the art and many will be damaged. Don't be afraid to turn down anything that could be dangerous – in the long run using hazardous equipment will backfire on you and the donating company
- **Accounting** – stock items and anything of value need to be accounted for and can't always be offset against Corporation tax. The good news is that special reliefs were introduced in 1991 for companies giving equipment to schools, colleges and higher education centres

Is it for you?

If you're not happy asking for donations, try asking for gifts in kind as an alternative.

Money for old rope

It's amazing what you can raise money from! Lots of people collect tin foil for Guide Dogs for the Blind but did you know recycling companies can help you raise money from petrol vouchers, computer printing cartridges, old photos and even knitting needles? Contact the Charities Aid Foundation (CAF) for more information (see the end of today).

Secondments

Recession and redundancy has had one benefit for the charitable sector, with increasing numbers of companies agreeing to second staff to charities to provide expert help.

Pros
- **Expert advice for free** – the seconded staff member remains on the company payroll, but comes to work for your charity, full or part time. A great way to get consistent expert advice and training in accountancy, business planning, marketing and PR etc.
- **The company employee's salary** (or a proportion of it if part time) is a tax deductible business expense

Cons
- **All secondments come to an end** – but with careful planning, they'll have trained your volunteers or staff, or solved the problem they were brought in to look at by then

Is it for you?
Could your cause use some expert advice? If you're contemplating recruiting a specialist in marketing, finance, IT or any other business discipline, a secondee might be an alternative solution.

Events

Fundraising events come in all shapes and sizes – from sponsored egg & spoon races to international sporting competitions and royal galas.

You can use just about every fundraising technique listed so far in conjunction with an event – sponsorship, donations, gifts in kind and promotions.

Examples
Ranging in size and fundraising capacity from

- Comic Relief Red Nose Day – a major event combining hundreds of independent events run by volunteers to

- every sponsored swim, silence, knit and bungee jump for which you have ever sponsored friends and children

Pros

- **PR** – events make great stories and photo calls for the press. Celebrity involvement can boost exposure too
- **Fun** – you can get up to all sorts of glamorous, exciting or just plain daft things in the name of charity. Pick who you want to get involved and choose your poison!
- **Mass involvement** – events mean lots of people, around the country or in one place. Either way, this means getting your message to a wider audience and publicising your cause
- **Tax concessions** apply to some small events such as fetes, jumble sales, concerts or sports events. Concessions may also apply to educational conferences designed to inform the audience about the cause's purpose (as long as it's charitable). Again check with the Inland Revenue before going ahead

Cons

- **Organisation** – the key to a good event is making it happen without effort on the day. That means enormous amounts of planning, attention to detail and hard work. Don't underestimate how much!
- **Cost** – putting on an event tends to cost money, for venues, insurance, publicity, equipment and materials ... the list is endless. Even if you do work on the beg, borrow and steal principle (well, legally appropriate anyway), you will still have to pay out money to raise it

- **Trading** – for larger events you may need to sell tickets and organise any trading taking place during the event through a separate non-charitable trading company. You then donate the profits you make back to the charity through a covenant or Gift Aid. Ask your tax office for advice

You may also be eligible for relief on VAT – again check with your local VAT office.

Small lotteries

Lotteries likely to make over £20,000 from ticket sales (you can't deduct the value of the prizes to slip under the net!) need a licence from the Gaming Board and are controlled by strict regulations.

You don't need a licence for a small lottery but you'll need to stick to certain conditions

- make sure the lottery's incidental to another event or activity
- run the whole thing during the event and on the same site – selling tickets, making the draw and announcing the result
- don't offer any cash prizes
- don't spend any more than £250 on prizes – but then again, hopefully they've all been donated!

Is it for you?
If you're running an event, lotteries create an excellent additional revenue stream, but you still need to get all the prizes donated.

Employee participation

More and more employees are being encouraged to participate in fundraising activities through their work. Events are a great morale booster, good fun and improve team spirit. Lots of companies also match donations raised by employees – doubling the reward of your effort.

ASDA, the supermarket chain, is one of many companies who have recently taken to naming a charity of the year. All their efforts – from sponsorship, donations and employee events – are concentrated on that one charity for 12 whole months. Get nominated and you're in for an exciting and profitable year!

On the quieter side, **Give as You Earn** schemes, where employees donate money straight from their wage packets before tax, are easy, painless and can be administered via the payroll system (with little hassle for the company).

Is it for you?
Large scale employee involvement is generally reserved for really popular causes – children, medical issues and so forth. You don't have to be a household name national charity, a cause with strong local appeal should also do well. If you have active supporters linked to a local company, ask them to do some investigating and see how much support they can drum up.

It's a great idea but...

Before you rush off to organise that fancy dress ball or get
your new book sponsored, consider your supporters. How
will they feel about your chosen approach? Remember,
alienate loyal supporters and you shoot yourself in the foot!
As well as giving a bad name to fundraisers everywhere.

Still searching for inspiration?

Check out the Charity Aid Foundation's (CAF) web site
in the Internet – http://www.charitynet.org

It gives up to date information on tax effective giving –
in the UK, Europe and the US (501c tax exempt
causes, for example charities, schools and
universities, bodies which are given charitable status
for fundraising purposes); the latest fundraising news;
and access to other Internet sites with news of
company charitable support around the world.

Summary

Today you've looked at the fundraising options and
hopefully discovered one you are confident you can
tackle. Now let's find a donor!

Spotting a donor

The donor hunt begins!

You should now know:

- what you need to fund and why
- why your project might appeal to a company

Now let's start the hunt for that elusive donor, remembering as we go the two crucial questions we asked on Sunday:

- what are you selling?
- why should a donor be interested?

Finding that crock of gold

A few words of caution. Any company listed as giving a good deal of financial support to charity will be inundated with appeals – often hundreds a week for the larger PLCs. Just because a company is seemingly profitable and successful doesn't mean they can automatically support your cause.

Success in corporate fundraising isn't simply finding a crock of gold at the end of a rainbow. You've got to find the right pot, with the right sort of label and then persuade the company to put your name on it!

Pereto's rule

Your dreams could come true and you could persuade one company to fund everything. More realistically, you're likely to need a range of donors able to give varying sizes of gifts to completely fund your project. During your search, bear in mind Pereto's rule.

More commonly applied to planning manufacturing, according to Pereto's rule you'll expend 80% of your effort achieving 20% of your work and vice versa. It's just as relevant to fundraising – you'll raise 80% of the money you need from 20% of your donors, and vice versa. In fact it can take just as much effort to raise £100 as it does to raise £100,000. Keep this in mind when deciding what potential a donor really has.

Where to look

Donors crop up in the most surprising places. So it's worth doing some innovative detective work. You can get an agency to do this – there are lots of reputable ones around – but their expertise doesn't come cheap, so be sure you are ready to make the investment.

All detectives have to start somewhere, so like the best Sherlock Holmes start by pulling together some key facts.

Tracking down the obvious donors

First make a list of obvious targets for donations. Start your
hunt by looking in the most obvious places:

- **your back yard** – what companies are based near your
  cause or project, or share the same catchment area?
- **the common interest club** – what companies are
  influenced by your cause's work or deal with the same
  subject matter? Companies that should fund you?
- **the back scratching club** – what companies
  supply goods or services to your cause? Everyone
  from specialist machine suppliers to your insurance
  company or solicitor
- **the hobby club** – any company producing goods or
  services of special interest to your supporters or
  those who benefit from your cause's work, e.g.
  gardening equipment for the National Trust;
  binoculars for the RNLI (Royal National Lifeboat
  Institution); tapestry kits for the Embroiderers' Guild
  and so on. These may be good targets for
  endorsements or promotions

The less obvious places

If at first you don't succeed, cast your net a little wider.
Some of the less obvious places to look include:

- **friends in need** – do you have any company
  directors on your board of trustees? What about
  their partners? Or your volunteers? Ask for help at

your next trustees' meeting or via your in-house
newsletter or notice board. These may also be the
best people to do the asking for you

- **community support** – check out who supports
other local causes. Look in the parish magazine,
local newspaper, take a snoop at the wall plaques in
local venues, or newsletters from other charities.
Ask your solicitor if he or she administers any trusts.

Remember, these benefactors may have reasons
other than local community interest for supporting
something. Don't presume they can help you, but
you could unearth a gold mine

- **hidden companies** – there will be companies you
never even knew existed – just look in the
telephone directory. Your local council offices or the
Chamber of Commerce may be able to give you a
list of companies in the area. Check company
guides like *Dun & Bradstreet* or *Who Owns Whom*
to see if there are larger company subsidiaries in
your area

- **charity lists** – charities and trusts are usually
registered at a central office – the Charity
Commission in the UK. See if you can search their
records, especially if they have computerised
systems making it easier to pinpoint trusts funding
particular needs

A morning surfing through these computer records
can turn up unlisted or newly registered trusts not
yet included in the published guides. Worth a trawl
if you're feeling lucky

Get really lateral

Put on your marketing hat and let your imagination run riot. Look at names, adverts, images, even music used by companies and see if these could link well with your charity. What about the Dulux dog for Battersea Dogs Home. Or Hamlet Cigars to fund a string quartet (playing Bach's Air on a G string of course!).

Checking out potential donors

Next check out each company's giving policy by looking in:

- **company giving guides** – generally dealing with larger more profitable companies, there are lots to choose from. The most reliable are those published by the Directory of Social Change and the Charity Commission (or equivalent bodies in your country). Published annually they outline company giving criteria – what they will and won't fund (causes/types of fundraising), how much they give and who to contact
- **trust giving guides** – the same thing for charitable trusts. Just to confuse the matter not all trusts linked to companies are named after the company – the Monument Trust is linked to the Sainsbury family of supermarket fame. Look out for clues such as shared officials and addresses

Then check out any information from the company itself via

- **company reports** – phone up and ask for a copy of the annual report. Some companies also publish separate corporate giving reports, containing more details about the projects they are actively involved in

- **your spy network!** – ask around to see if your friends, colleagues or volunteers know what the company supports (and doesn't). This could provide vital clues if the company is coy about what it will and won't fund in the official guide, and for smaller local companies that may not be listed. You may find some very useful routes into the company just by talking to these contacts

Priority hit lists

Remove any company that doesn't fund your general cause. Don't bother asking for funds for a donkey sanctuary if the company only supports medical research, it only wastes their time and yours. Then go back through all the names you've come up with and rank them from 1-3

1 **hot prospect** – high giving potential with good contacts; great match with your cause/project ... why hadn't you thought of them before?
2 **middle runners** – a good match but maybe your contacts aren't great or they only give small gifts. Ones to ask but don't expect the earth
3 **rank outsider** – smallest giving potential; tenuous links to your cause. Worth a try but catch them on a good day!

Getting advice – a who's who

The next step is to go straight to the horse's mouth. Make some preliminary enquiries by talking to whoever handles the charitable budget you're trying to tap into. Up springs a new problem – who on earth do you talk to?

On Sunday we mentioned that there are lots of different places inside a company that may have funds to give to charity. So where can you look?

- **Charitable donations administration** – possibly handled by a trust administrator for companies with separate trusts, the Company Secretary or, in smaller companies, one of the directors. You'll probably identify a name to contact from the corporate giving guides
- **Marketing departments** – with budgets to help promote their product, sometimes available at short notice, these are potential targets for sponsorship or promotions
- **Personnel or Human Resources departments** – for projects that could be used to train staff. Some – The Rank Organisation for example – may even have budgets to help you train your staff
- **Staff associations or trade unions** – these may have money to give out from their own fundraising activities, or access to funds by nominating causes to their trade union HQ

Finally don't forget your moles – your contacts who know someone senior in the prospect company. We look at what to do with them in a moment.

Things to find out

Research and list of potential targets firmly under your belt, it's time to leap in the deep end and make your first contact. Before you go to all the effort of putting together a proposal establish whether or not it's worthwhile.

The simplest approach is for you or your mole to pick up the phone or pen a brief letter. Ask whether or not the company would consider a proposal from your sort of cause and project. Keep things general and try to avoid backing yourself into a corner where the only answer is an emphatic 'No!' or 'Get lost!'.

Check if you are in touch with the right person or if you should contact someone else. Don't get into details – save that for your proposal. There's nothing more irritating than someone rambling on about how worthy and desperate their cause is. Save lecturing for the pulpit!

The paranoia syndrome

Some fundraisers get paranoid about rejection. It's par for the course in fundraising but don't let it make you scared of asking. If you've identified the right sort of company with the right criteria you're helping everyone by asking these questions now. It can even help you identify new sources of funds or proposal ideas you hadn't even thought of.

Get one of your trustees or contacts (your mole) to make these enquiries for you and you may avoid the pain of direct rejection. Brief these contacts really well, otherwise you can end up with the blind leading the blind...

The secret of timing

Great timing is crucial. Ask for support too late, the company funds may already be promised to someone else; send it in too early, you may have to wait months for the next meeting. If the company does sound interested in your project find out the following details:

- **how far ahead are company funds committed?** some companies distribute their budgets annually, maybe up to 12 months in advance
- **when does the company consider appeals?** it's not uncommon for companies to consider donations annually or perhaps four times a year, although marketing budgets may be more readily accessible. There may be a pile of appeals waiting to be considered, so if yours is at the bottom, it's anyone's guess as to when it will emerge for consideration
- **when do they need to have your appeal?** if papers are collated or distributed before a September meeting, you may need to send them in at the end of July. Find out when the submission deadline is

Also check what the company wants you to provide. This is one of the things you'll think about tomorrow when you put together your proposal.

What to do about company benefits

The last thing to think about today is what benefits you are able to give. After all, this may well dictate the sort of fundraising approach you can make.

Now that you have a list of possible companies to approach, think carefully about the sorts of benefits you could offer. Don't promise the earth – after all you don't want to spend your hard earned sponsorship money on wining and dining the company.

If you're not sure what to offer, check out what other charities similar to yours do. Above all believe you do have something to offer, but be realistic. Here are some thoughts to get your imagination going.

Top 10 benefits

Here are some suggestions for benefits you could offer a company ... for the right money!

1 **PR and media coverage** – everything from the national press to local papers and radio stations.
2 **In-house publicity** – produce articles for company magazines as well as your own publications.
3 **On-site recognition** – plaques; logos on event brochures or publications; attending photo calls; company display stands at events.
4 **Special access** to your events or facilities (including for employees and customers).
5 **Access to speakers** or performers for company events.
6 **Training** – clearing a graveyard? Get companies to use it as a management team-building project.

7 **Services** – campaigning for the environment? Offer to advise the company as to how it can be greener.

8 **Advance booking** for your cause's events or products, a good way to get bums on seats if you run regular events.

9 **Access to your facilities** for entertainment – if you're saving a church, mansion or park could it be used for corporate entertainment at any time?

10 **Corporate membership** – a simple scheme where members get special access to all the above benefits in return for regular annual support.

A cautionary tale

The British Government recently got caught in a compromising situation due to their fundraising efforts.

The Observer newspaper reported that the Premier Club, a Conservative party dining club, was offering members the chance to invite the Prime Minister and Cabinet colleagues as guest speakers to private dinners for the business community. No problem there.

Prospective club members were advised, however, that they could declare their donations (of £10,000 or £100,000) as entertainment expenses, to avoid revealing that this sum was in effect a donation to Conservative party funds. Under the Companies Act, all donations must be declared in company accounts, or directors can be liable to a fine.

The moral of this story is quite simple. Strive to be utterly legal, decent and honest – especially if you run a lobbying group without charitable status. If supporters choose to give money to you, that's great, but make sure everything is declared.

Anaesthetics are dangerous!

A final thought. Asking a donor too soon for too little can anaesthetise them for years. Once someone has given, they may feel they've done their bit and someone else should chip in. In general, a cool-off period of a year to 18 months is advisable before asking someone to support you again.

So beware of asking that multi-millionaire you've kept up your sleeve all these months for a few hundred pounds, when they might be happy to give you £1 million! Find out what other commitments they have. Bide your time and show them the big picture. They still may only come up with £100, but at least you've given them the option.

Summary

Today you've drawn up a list of companies that look like good prospects. You've :

- checked out their giving criteria
- found out what sort of fundraising they'll support
- established when they consider proposals and give out funds
- made your first contact to see if the company would consider your proposal

You've also thought about what benefits you can reasonably offer the company if considering a commercial link up.

Tomorrow you put together that all important proposal.

Putting together your appeal

Today all your hard work this week comes to fruition. Start the day by pulling together all the facts and figures you've collected since Sunday. These are what you will use to create your appeal proposal.

Finding the perfect formula

There are no hard and fast rules about what you can and can't put in a fundraising proposal. If someone had come up with the perfect formula they would doubtless have patented it and now be sunning themselves on a beach in the Seychelles!

Obviously, there are certain things you must be sure to say. Namely the facts you gathered together on Monday to prove your need:

- what is your cause and why is it important?
- what you want to do – a brief explanation of your project

- what you need in order to do it

which leads you neatly to

- the request – how you want the prospect donor to help

Cover these points clearly and concisely and you are well on the way to having a good convincing appeal.

Face to face appeals

There may be occasions when you don't need to present a formal written appeal, especially if you or a supporter are asking a donor for support face to face.

It's still worth working through what should go in a written proposal just to get your argument straight. Then you'll have all the facts and figures at your fingertips. That proves you've considered all the options and is far more convincing than having to stammer 'Well..er.. that's a very interesting question. I'll have to come back to you on that'!

It's the way I tell 'em

Armed with the skeleton of your appeal story, now think about presentation. Different approaches will appeal to different companies and be suited to different types of fundraising. Think about the image you want to convey and adapt your appeal, and the tone of voice you use, to fit.

Take a leaf out of the following charities' books and try one of these approaches:

The hard facts
If the company is clearly interested in your cause and not concerned about promotional benefits, try telling it like it is.

The RSPCA often resorts to shock tactics, using pictures of starving, mistreated animals. The information is shocking but generates the support required. As their Head of Campaigns Kate Parminter puts it:

> *an advert that doesn't get any complaints is frankly too anodyne.*

Think positive
If your cause is a subject people like avoiding, package it up by focusing on positive solutions.

Millions of people around the world suffer from depression, but it's not something many people like to admit. The charity Defeat Depression used a fun run to raise awareness, highlight how exercise could help defeat depression, and to raise funds too.

The complementary approach
If the company you're targeting is interested in promotional benefits, try using the cause to complement the promotion.

Border Fine Arts, a porcelain figurine manufacturer specialising in wildlife and bird statuettes, linked up with the RSPB's Campaign for the Countryside to promote their figures of barn owls, martins and other rare British countryside birds.

Let's have a party
Famine in Africa and AIDS are not subjects that provoke joy and excitement. And yet, that's exactly what the Live Aid and Freddie Mercury benefit concerts did, bringing together thousands of fans wanting a party whilst raising funds for two of the most devastating problems of the twentieth century.

Comic Relief continues that same principle. You can raise funds for emotive and serious subjects, get the message across and have great fun at the same time.

One compulsory rule

Everyone loves getting a cheque but the funds you raise don't simply become yours to do with as you please. Donors give money for a specific purpose, so that's how you've got to use it: not to pay for some other pipe-dream, no matter how worthy.

If your original project falls through, you must ask the donor if you can use the money for another purpose. Fail to do this, you're defrauding the donor. Slapped wrists all round if you get caught.

So what if you raise more money than planned? It can happen! Again, technically you must ask permission to use the money for another project, but you can save yourself the headache by planning ahead.

Numerous appeals explain that the money raised will be used to support the specific project and the general purposes of the charity. Then excess funds can be used to support the charity's work as a whole. Telling donors you've funded an additional project too then becomes an added bonus.

It's still worth telling major donors if their money came after you reached your initial target. Apart from being polite, it's a good way to build trust and maybe further support.

Are you within the law?

Stating the purpose for which money is being raised up front may not be the only regulation with which you need to comply.

Most countries have strict laws about raising money for charity – in the UK it's set out in the 1994 Charities Act. Rather than risk a policeman knocking at your door just as the curtain rises on your benefit premiere, check now.

I'M PLEASED TO ANNOUNCE...

The UK Charities Act is designed to protect donors and make it clear what their donations are used for. Some of the additional things you need to think about include:

- telling prospective donors if they're being asked for
  support by a *professional fundraiser* as defined by
  the Act. A professional fundraiser is someone who
  raises money for charity wholly or primarily for their
  own gain, receiving more than £500 payment to do
  so – perhaps someone you contract from an
  agency or a freelance fundraiser
  - this doesn't apply to charity employees on the
    payroll. It's really a way of protecting the donor
    from being duped – how would you feel if a
    neighbour sold you a car and only afterwards told
    you he was a car dealer?

- if you or any commercial business (defined in the
  UK Charities Act as a *commercial participator*) sell
  goods to benefit a charity, you must state how much
  of the purchase price will go to that good cause –
  on the product and wherever you sell it (from
  adverts to shop stands or stalls)

Rather than hope for the best, contact the Charity
Commission (or equivalent body in Europe or the US),
and ask for any guidance notes they produce.

10 optional rules for appeals

Once you've determined your basic argument and tone of
voice, what else should you consider? As we've said there
are no hard and fast rules. However, you may want to
consider these tips as you create your own masterpiece.

Do

1 **Keep it short** – one side of A4 plus your budget if possible.
2 **Keep to the point** – we need funds for our donkey sanctuary to build a new stable. Not 'six years ago this little old lady came to me with this cute donkey she couldn't care for any more, so we decided to take care of it and ... and' ... yawn, yawn.
3 **Be clear what you're asking for** – if you don't tell the donor you need money or equipment, you can't expect them to be clairvoyant!
4 **Send what you are asked for** – some companies just want a brief letter. Others will have special requests – duplicate copies, lists of your trustees, sales leaflets about the equipment etc. Check first and send the right information

and if you're asked to send a highly detailed appeal

5 **Include an Executive summary** – a single page encapsulating your appeal, for directors in a hurry!

Then there are certain things that are best avoided at all costs.

Don't

6 **Send exploding appeal packages** that shower bits of paper everywhere ... they will go straight in the bin!
7 **Be too glossy** – be smart and business-like but don't go overboard or donors will think you have money to burn.

8 **Over-do the widgets** – if you're enticing a
company into a promotion, an exemplary widget
may be just the thing. Sending gold-plated credit
card holders when you need money to stop your
building falling down will win no prizes.

9 **Forget the budget** – no matter how emotive your
letter, if the figures aren't clear don't expect a
company to invest in you.

10 **Undersell yourself** – your need is real, so don't be
too self-effacing and do yourself down.

The budget sheet

Once you've proved your case and explained what you
want to do, it's time to pull together the budget.

Look back at the budget you and your team produced on
Monday. There are two possible types of budgets you can
now develop to present to a company

1 The shopping list budget

This prices everything you need to make your project a reality – from equipment and buildings to salaries, training costs and those all important administration costs.

Shopping list budgets are best suited to straightforward donation appeals, or as back-up to organising employee fundraising drives: wherever you're trying to reach a specific funding target.

2 The added value budget

This combines your specific shopping list with a price for the added value of the link with your cause's name or logo. This promotional cost is perceived rather than real, but totally justified for sponsorships, events or any link-up where the company benefits from being promoted alongside your cause's logo or name.

Many charities put a price tag on their logo, for larger high profile charities sometimes thousands of pounds. The actual amount is up to your cause, but if you decide to price your logo stick to that value. Never sell it cheap!

Fundraising events

Here you'll need to produce a new budget – one that covers all the event costs and the added value price tag for linking up with your logo.

A word of warning. It's frightening how many well intentioned events run way over budget (as you try to get every last detail right) and end up costing the cause money rather than raising it. Be ultra realistic and aim to cover all your costs before you sell a single ticket. The tickets are your profit stream.

Don't forget the VAT

Finally, if you're producing a budget for a commercial link up, don't forget to add the VAT (if applicable).

Benefits

If you're after commercial support (rather than a donation) next come the benefits of supporting your project. Obvious ones can be set in stone – a sponsor's logo on a theatre programme cover, mailings to all your members (those all important potential customers). Some, however, may come to you later.

Say what the benefits can include, citing the key ones, but leave yourself room for manoeuvre. Wait until you get a bite and then sit down with the sponsor to discuss suitable benefits. You've already established what you can reasonably provide, and some companies will want far less than you anticipate. Others will suggest ideas you've never thought of, so at that stage, you can react to opportunity.

Finishing touches

Now that your appeal has taken shape, a few final tips before you pop it in the post box.

Top tips

Just before you seal that appeal envelope, check:

- **is everything legal, decent and honest?** Elaborating the truth can get you into trouble, with the prospect company and the law. The need is real so you shouldn't need to exaggerate to get people interested
- **have you set an end date for the appeal?** It focuses people's minds and encourages prospect donors to respond by a set date. It'll also help keep your fundraising efforts on track
- **is it clear who you're raising funds for?** If not put your cause's name up front

- **if you're raising funds for someone else**, a local branch for the parent charity for example, you need the parent charity's permission to do this and an agreement as to how and when money raised will be passed to the beneficiary charity. This is especially important if you're raising money for good causes like schools, health or local authority care services, which aren't always legally charities but are generally treated as such by the tax man
- **have you suggested a visit or a meeting?** Conveying all you need to in one letter is, as you've discovered, very hard. Why not invite the donor to come and visit your project? Or offer to meet them to discuss the project in more detail? The company will only take you up on the offer if they're interested, but at least you've extended the invitation
- **you left your appeal overnight?** It's easy to get too close to an appeal to see the mistakes – spelling, facts, your prospect's name. Leave your letter overnight and read it with fresh eyes in the morning – at the RSPB this stopped an appeal going out asking for funds to save the Great White Shark ... rather than the Great White Stork!
- **the personal touch** – people like to feel special, so a personalised letter, even if in reality we know it's probably one of a hundred similar appeal letters, can make all the difference. If you're doing a mass mailing, check all the details apply to the company you're contacting; if you or a supporter know the company contact fairly well, why not personalise the letter with a friendly greeting or a hand-written PS?

Summary

The moment of truth

Today, you've pulled together all the analysis and plans you've have made since Sunday and come up with what, hopefully, will be a winning appeal. Above all, by taking time to do your homework and pinpoint how to approach the right prospect in the right way, you've eliminated as much risk as possible from the fundraising process.

Oh, one final thought. If you have attractive handwriting, try hand addressing the envelope. Many company letters will simply be screened by secretaries, however any added touch is worth it. If you have any doubts about this ploy, just consider which letters you open first thing in the morning? The brown type-written envelopes, or the interesting looking hand-written white ones?

Only two things left to do today. Pop your appeal in the post and firmly cross your fingers.

Decisions, decisions

You woke up this morning hoping for a decision, however you'll have to be patient. This morning you may discover there is more work to do and you haven't seen the last of your appeal.

Pitches and amending your appeal

Some companies may react to your appeal by asking to meet to discuss your proposal. This doesn't mean they're about to give you a blank cheque, but it does mean you're in with a good chance of getting their support.

Take BT. In 1995 they gave more than £15m in charitable support ... but received more than 200 appeals for donations or sponsorship every week. Any company that takes the time to meet you and find out more is obviously interested in what you do.

Use the time well, as a chance to adapt your appeal to suit their needs too. Maybe you've asked for a donation but the company is more interested in sponsorship or a promotion. See if you can accommodate each other, although never subjugate the project's needs to those of the company. After all, that's not why you're trying to raise funds!

The icing on the cake

Remember your invitation to visit? What happens if the company says yes? Again, this is a pretty good indication that they're interested. So make sure you show them what they need to see.

Show them how things are now ... including the bad bits. Marion Alford, Appeal Director for the Great Ormond Street Children's Hospital Wishing Well Appeal used some very strange routes when she showed prospective donors around the hospital. They'd go via back corridors where the walls were crumbling. The GOS staff concentrated on explaining what they wanted to do – the problems were self-evident as they walked down the corridor.

Don't do all the talking yourself either. The people on the front line – carers, reserve wardens, teachers, volunteers – know what the job entails and are often the most persuasive lobbyists available to you.

That goes for the beneficiaries of your cause's work too. There are few things more emotive than seeing the positive results of past work – handicapped children learning new skills, animals recovering from ill-treatment, restored buildings or performances by artistic groups. Let your existing work demonstrate what you could do ... given the funds.

Parallel lobbying

Whether or not you get the chance to speak to the company direct, it may be worth getting others to do some lobbying on your behalf.

Do you have an existing supporter well placed to mention that your appeal is worth considering? Alternatively, if you have lots of supporters who are employees of the company and willing to do some employee fundraising on your behalf, make sure their bosses get to hear about this as your appeal letter hits the relevant director's desk.

Don't pressurise the company, but a well timed word in the right person's ear could make a company look at your appeal in a new light.

Getting to yes

There will come a point where you simply need an answer. Sadly, not every company answers appeal letters. Many work on the basis that if you hear nothing by a certain date, they can't help. This is fair enough if you consider the number of rejection letters they could have to send out (not to mention the time and expense).

If there is no cut off date set by the company, follow up your appeal request. Again, there are no hard and fast rules. Simply call the person you sent the appeal to, or get your mole to ask their contact in the company.

Check that the appeal letter arrived – things do go astray – and if it's being considered on a certain date. When too many appeals are earmarked for one company committee meeting, it's not uncommon for some to be re-scheduled for consideration at the next meeting.

If this delay means the difference between your project
going ahead or failing, explain this. It may be possible to
get an interim indication of whether your appeal is likely to
succeed – this may help to persuade others to give too,
even if it can't speed up the receipt of a cheque from the
company in question.

Getting to No

Sometimes it takes an eternity to get a response. There may
even come a point when you feel your time is being
wasted. People are often as shy of turning down appeals as
they are to ask for money. So if endless calls are never
returned or you're always fobbed off with a 'Yes, it's being
considered' but no-one will commit to a decision date, you
may need to force one.

If you do go back to the company and ask for a firm yes or
no, always stay polite. Corporate indecision may simply
result from having to negotiate too much red tape, despite
the company being keen to help. Stay polite and you may
yet win that vital support.

The final decision

When that fateful final decision does come, what then?

What to do with rejection

Above all stay philosophical. You still need to raise the
money, so maybe you can learn something from your
efforts:

- **don't think of it as your failure** – 90% of fundraising is knocking on closed doors. So keep your spirits up. Don't brood over the doors you can't prise open, celebrate the ones you do!

- **thank companies for their consideration** – always stay polite. If the rejection was a nice one, drop the company a line in due course to keep them informed about your work (maybe a couple of times a year). The timing of your appeal may not have been right and you can always ask for support for another appeal on another day
- **ask their advice** – if appropriate and you have a good existing relationship with the company but they just couldn't help this time, maybe they can advise you as to where to find alternative help. They may also be able to give you guidance as to how to strengthen your appeal
- **if the rejection was uncompromising** (you'll know if it was less than friendly!) decide whether to ignore it or look for other company contacts to educate

- **if the company** is a prospect who you identified as being one that should support your cause, it may be time to try interesting another target, employees rather than board directors for example

What to do with success

We'll look at the longer term things you can do with success tomorrow, but today's response is to:

- **thank the company** – immediately! You'd be amazed how often fundraisers forget. Even if ultimately the official thanks should come from the head of the charity (especially for large donations),whoever made the appeal should pick up the phone or write a quick note thanking the company for their support . Reply by return whenever possible. Personalise your thanks, tailoring it to the company. If the cheque came with a hand written note, send a hand written note back. Be grateful, but appropriate – boot licking in response to a £100 donation will make you seem facetious!
- **agree any conditions** on future use of the donation – hopefully there won't be any but it's advisable to be absolutely clear from the start. Hospitals may at some stage want to sell on out of date equipment. Make sure the donor is happy with this before grabbing the equipment and running!
- **celebrate it!** – an awful lot of hard work from a lot of people goes into fundraising. When you achieve success, share it with everyone involved. Apart from boosting morale, a pat on the back now can persuade people to do a great deal more for you in the future. And that's a matter of life and death when it comes to organising events!

Getting it all in writing

Once the euphoria of success has subsided a bit, let's get back to reality. Gentlemen's agreements are all well and good, but there are an awful lot of dishonourable gentlemen … and ladies out there!

Don't presume everyone is as nice and helpful as you are! If you enter into any commercially based fundraising deal – sponsorship or promotion/endorsement – put together a contract or letter of agreement setting out all the details of the deal.

Things to include in an agreement letter

Try to cover all the following points in your letter of agreement:

- **terms** – how much money and how it will be collected/paid to you, percentage payment per product sold and so on

- **an outline** of who from your cause and the company is responsible for what
- **a timetable** – including start and finish dates, payment dates, planning or reporting deadlines
- **date for a review meeting** – especially for promotions to decide whether to renew/extend the deal
- **a get out clause** – stating that you can prevent future use or exploitation of your name if you are not fully satisfied with the way things have gone – especially if your cause's name has been misrepresented

Put simply, lay out your basic plans in a formal letter to which both parties agree and sign. Check with The Institute of Charity Fundraising Managers (ICFM) or whoever represents fundraisers nationally to see if they have any model contract forms.

Housekeeping

Next, put a few pieces of housekeeping in place, to ensure the money you've raised is properly managed. For example:

- account for special appeal funds separately – keep your own records of all the money you've raised and when it is paid in
- set up a separate bank account – if you're raising money for a parent charity, or a one off cause (like the church roof) which doesn't have an existing charity bank account, so the funds don't just disappear into the charity pot. Events too, where you need to keep trading money entirely separate from donations and general charity funds

Getting the project going

The final and most important point is to set the project in motion. You can tackle the hard work next week but these are some of the things you may need to do:

Donations
Once you've reached the target, this is a straightforward matter. Simply tell the charity the money is in the bank and off you go (although doubtless you now have another complex job ahead, organising the project itself!).

Sponsorships
If the company agreed to a sponsorship, now you need to fulfil all those agreed benefits. Look back at the list you agreed with the company. Make sure both parties are happy with the schedule and try to get ahead of the game by collecting PR material such as logo bromides, style sheets explaining how to reproduce the logo, and plan any media activity.

Promotions and endorsements
The cause and the company now need to get together to approve packaging and widget design, confirm copy and plan any PR or media activity linked to launching the promotion or endorsement.

Events and employee participation
Here the work is only just beginning! Once the funding is in place, your attention must move to organising the actual event, making detailed plans, getting volunteers in place, arranging publicity, selling tickets (if required) and generally getting the show on the road. But that's another story!

Summary

Today you've tried your level best to promote your appeal and, if necessary, adapt it so it is more attractive to the company. Hopefully, you're now celebrating your success and planning for the future. Even if you are commiserating because the company declined to support you, the best fundraisers will live to fight another day – tomorrow.

Making the most of your week

Whatever decision the prospect company reached yesterday, today you take a quick look back and then to the future. This week you've:

- taken a long hard look at your cause
- decided what fundraising method would work for you
- investigated who might support you and why
- put together an appeal and
- tailored the appeal to attract the right support

So, what next?

Making the most of success

Successful fundraising doesn't stop with putting the cheque in the bank. Once you've attracted funding you need to build on your relationship with the company and say some longer term thank yous. This doesn't just mean fulfilling the benefits you've agreed. It's about building strong bonds and partnerships for the future, and nurturing them. You will have at least a year (the period of time most funding deals last) to do this. Here are some of the things you can do:

- **send regular reports** – whatever type of funding you've been given, it's supporting a specific project. Send the company regular reports to show what they are helping to fund – you can fill in more detail about your cause's work, get the company more involved and hopefully thoroughly convert them to the cause by the end of the year

- **spread the thanks around** – it costs nothing to say thank you but can influence a lot of people. Judge how much you do by the proportionate size of the support (a large donation from some companies may be comparatively small for others).
  - Thank the donor wherever you can – in editorials, annual reports, on plaques on equipment or buildings. You can even name a building after a really major donor
- **get the company involved** – support is an excuse to build greater involvement. Invite the company directors down to see the work they've funded in progress. Offer to give a talk to the company staff association or write an article for their staff magazine. This is your chance to get your cause involved with as many aspects of the company as possible, always presuming this is a sensible use of your time and resources.

Reviewing success

Even success is something that should be reflected upon. Throughout the time the company supports you, keep reviewing what works and what doesn't (including what the company thinks too). For sponsorships, you can use this information to put together an end of term report on the project.

Reviewing things will help you learn how to manage donors, sponsorships and promotional deals better in the future. It may also give you some ideas as to how the donor relationship could be enhanced to benefit both – a useful perspective if you come to put together a renewed appeal next year.

Making the most of rejection

The best way to handle rejection is also to learn from it.
Look back at the process you've been through this week
and see where things could be improved. Could your
appeal have been shorter or clearer? Was the cause or
project simply too fringe to be of interest?

The reasons for rejection could have been beyond your
control. Maybe the company's funds were fully committed
or another appeal beat you to the post. There's little you
can do about this except improve your timing.

Keep trying, but target your appeals even more carefully.
Some causes – like textile conservation or research into ME
(myalgic encephalomyelitis – disparagingly known as
yuppie flu) – no matter how important, are very specialised
and won't attract mainstream support.

Also consider whether your cause is well enough known.

You may simply need to raise the profile of the cause to get some support.

Making the most of the media

Whether you won or lost, media coverage can help raise your cause's profile, and hopefully attract more support. After all, it's quite common for prospect donors to be reluctant to be the first person to give but to be keen to join a party.

If you were successful and gained company support, shout it from the rooftops (check first that the company is happy for you to do this). Local papers thrive on stories about charities raising vital funds – but why stop there? If you can create any newsworthy or eye-catching story try contacting:

- **fundraising magazines** – read by fund givers as well as fundraisers

- **business journals** relevant to the company supporting you – or even the cause you're trying to raise money for
- **local radio and TV** – always on the look out for unusual stories, community fundraising activities, and photo opportunities when celebrities attend events or visit projects
- **specialist magazines** – the Textile Conservation Centre went about heightening its profile by getting coverage in interior design and collectors magazines like Interiors, Country Life and Hali (the definitive publication for antique carpet collectors)
- **national newspaper picture desks** – many broadsheet newspapers run regular picture features with unusual eye-catching images. If your cause is doing something photogenic, give them a call

However you attract media attention, be clear what you want them to say. If you decide to announce an appeal remember, this is something you can only usefully do once. People get bored of being asked again and again for money, so be sure to save a media appeal for funds for the right time and purpose.

Also remember that column inches in newspapers are a massive PR benefit for companies who want public recognition. So keep your clippings and make sure the funding company sees them too.

After the ball is over ...

After all the hubbub of fundraising, some of the following situations commonly crop up. Here are a few suggestions as to how to cope.

Insufficient funds
Sadly, you're obliged to return these to the donor unless you've already specified in the appeal literature what would happen in this case.

- If the donor doesn't want their money back you need to get them to sign a disclaimer
- If you can't identify the donor, make sure you've made every effort to trace them, publicising what has happened in your newsletter or local paper for example. Who knows, this may even prompt some benefactor to reach into their wallet and give you the shortfall
- Any money left over needs to be set up in a special charitable account, something the national body representing charities in your country will have to organise for you. Get in touch and ask for advice

Transferring funds to other projects
Don't do it! Conveniently transferring funds to another project because the original one was cancelled or just because you feel like it, is not legal. (Look back at Thursday if you need reminding.) Explain the situation to the donor and take it from there.

Raised too much money
Congratulations! Once you've celebrated a bit, back to reality.

- If you didn't state in your appeal literature what surplus funds would be used for, go back to the donor and get their permission to use their money for another project. Again, get a disclaimer or note from them stating their agreement

- Otherwise, it's back to the Charity Commission (or equivalent body) to check whether or not you'll need a special scheme to enable you to use the money for your cause

Raising a little extra – getting close to your target
This is a great incentive to give just a little bit more. If you're a hair's breadth from the amount you need, try phoning round your best donors – or those who have given much less than anticipated. You can never expect a larger donation but it's worth asking for just a little bit more.

Raising a little extra – advertising
A great way to raise additional money from an event or publication is by asking companies to take out adverts in the publication or programme. Especially if you have any blank pages to fill.

Alternatively think really big like the NSPCC. Get a company to sponsor a TV ad. Daddies Ketchup, an HP Foods brand, have sponsored the NSPCC's TV ads for a couple of years. The ad includes a simple message of thanks to Daddies Sauce along the bottom of the screen, but most importantly helps the NSPCC get their message into millions of homes across the UK.

It's easy to create lots of levels of involvement from one line greetings for £20, a full page gold advert for several hundred, to filmed adverts for thousands, although you'll have to charge VAT if applicable .

When it comes to sorting out the details, if you don't speak the language – bromides, artwork, separations, pan tones – save yourself a headache and get someone who does to handle it all for you!

The end of a long week

Fundraising is hard work whether you are after a donation or a corporate deal. This week you've got to grips with some of the basic things you can do to make the task that little bit easier and hopefully improve your chances of success.

At the end of the day nothing beats finding a company with a good match to your cause. Nonetheless, luck will always play its part.

Pat White of the Notting Hill Housing Association, a fundraiser with more than 20 years success under her belt, puts it in perspective:

> *I get phone calls from other housing associations all the time asking for advice – but even I don't know after all this time what will work and what won't.*

There will always be times when the rules can be broken and companies that apparently have no intention of funding your sort of cause can be persuaded to do so. It only takes a director who is personally affected by your cause, a word in the right place...

So one final word on fundraising and sponsorship in a week. You can make plans and try your hardest to do things 'the right way', but when a little bit of luck comes along grab that chance and go with the flow. Nothing ventured, nothing gained.

Finding out more book list –

Direct Mail in a week – Liz Ferdi *Hodder and Stoughton*

Public Relations in a week – Claire Austin *Hodder and Stoughton*

Relationship Fundraising – Ken Burnett *The White Lion Press* – big gift fundraising from individuals

Teach yourself fundraising – Tony Elischer –*Hodder Headline*

Charity Appeals Directory of Social Change – Marion Alford – a major tome explaining how Great Ormond Street Children's Hospital ran their hugely successful Wishing Well Appeal. Probably the definitive analysis of how to run a major capital fundraising campaign – well worth the read.